Demoli

Strongholds

Evangelism and strategic-level spiritual warfare

by
Andii Bowsher
Priest in Charge of All Souls' Living Church, Halifax, and Chaplain of Calderdale College

GROVE BOOKS LIMITED
Bramcote   Nottingham   NG9 3DS

CONTENTS

THE COVER PICTURE

is by the author

AUTHOR'S NOTE

This booklet could not have been produced without the help and encouragement of my wife. I would also like to acknowledge a debt of gratitude to the members of my past and present churches for their help and prayer. This booklet is dedicated to them.

FURTHER READING

I particularly recommend the Walter Wink books for those who can cope with graduate theology! The first one is at the time of writing the only one likely to be found in this country. It is published by Fortress Press (1984) and called *Naming the Powers*.

For a balanced and thoroughly orthodox view of this and related subjects Nigel Wright's *The Fair Face of Evil* (Marshall Pickering, 1989) is much to be recommended.

The average reader will find John Dawson's *Taking our Cities for God* (Word, 1989) helpful. I would also recommend Peter Wagner's *Warfare Prayer* (Monarch 1992). This recommendation is with the proviso that Wagner fails to grapple with the central thesis of Wink's work. He simply writes it off as (I assume) liberal. Thus he fails to distinguish the difference between the Powers and the demonic.

First Impression February 1993

ISSN 0953-4946

ISBN 1 85174 231 X

1. INTRODUCTION

If you had picked up a book on spiritual warfare before the mid-1980s the chances are that you would have read about 'the world, the flesh and the devil' and how they impinge upon the life of the individual Christian. Since the mid-1980s it has been much more certain that you would read about 'principalities and powers'. It would be more likely that you would be told about how to go about identifying the spirits that may have the power to take authority in specific locations. You would also probably be told how to take authority over them so that evangelism could take place effectively.

The present situation

Spiritual warfare is now very much on the agenda in many churches. It seems to be an integral part of the upsurge of prayer which has been recently fostered by such things as the Marches for Jesus, Days of prayer for Revival and 'Prayer Combat days'. Much of the fostering activity has had particular theological slants in its approach to spiritual warfare. Such slants inevitably affect the way people pray; quite often encouraging them to address principalities and powers directly in speech. We must also acknowledge the impact of such novels as Frank Peretti's *This Present Darkness* and *Piercing the Darkness* for raising consciousness in evangelical churches with regard to spiritual warfare. His contribution is to be commended for making it plain that our struggle is at different levels and the decisive one is spiritual. The peril of popularization-by-novel is that artistic licence may be mistaken for gospel truth and inappropriate models of thought and action drawn from it.

In the first flush of charismatic renewal the Church was seen as 'the body of Christ'. More lately a tendency has grown to see it as 'the army of God'. Although this is not a particularly scriptural term the military imagery has been able to give some churches a way to talk of discipline and working together for the kingdom of God. It also gives a way to see Christian life and growth in active and dynamic terms. pushing back the frontiers of evil, working with God to extend his kingdom etc. It may be that the growing popularity of the metaphor of the army of God has fed the burgeoning awareness of spiritual warfare. In God's providence this awareness may be good, but we need to be vigilant as to the possible dangers of a wrong approach to 'principalities and powers'.

The aim and scope of this booklet

It is with this in mind that this booklet is written. Stated positively the aim is to examine how we should deal 'with principalities, with powers, with spiritual forces of evil in the heavenly realms' (Eph. 6.12) in such a way that the gospel may be more effectively communicated and the church grow. It is the conviction of the writer that spiritual warfare is a part of our evangelism and *vice versa*. It is important, therefore, that we aim for a balanced approach which will bring the most fruit for the Kingdom of God in the long run.

The author's assumptions

It is assumed that spiritual forces exist; that they have intelligence and will and that they are hell-bent on marring and destroying human welfare, especially human spiritual welfare. For these reasons they oppose the spread of the gospel. It will not be the place of this booklet to argue the existence of such forces. It is also assumed that the wisest source of information about these forces is scripture.

It is important to understand that we are not dealing in this booklet with what might be termed 'personal demons' but with what I am calling 'principalities and powers'. 'Personal demons' are spiritual entities which afflict individual human personalities. I take it that principalities and powers are to do with the social dimensions of human existence. Therefore this booklet is not about deliverance ministry and demonization.[1]

Pitfalls in dealing with the subject

It is very easy for treatments of spiritual warfare and related matters to run ahead of the scriptural evidence. One finds sometimes quite big theories based on only a small statement. For example, the prophecy against the king of Tyre in Ezekiel 28 is used to deduce the prehistory of Lucifer. While it may be true that this passage seems to be using the king of Tyre as a type of a spiritual being we must be a little less ready to conclude that it necessarily gives us doctrinal material about the forces of darkness. It may be that Ezekiel is being led to see the physical ruler of Tyre in terms of a story about the fall of a spiritual being. Such does not necessarily imply that the story is being endorsed as being historically true. What we may legitimately deduce is that there is a spiritual dimension to the reign of the king which seems to involve the subversion of God-given authority and that there is a parallel between the seen and the unseen dimensions of Tyre's ruler. We may, on other grounds, decide that the kind of picture that is painted of Lucifer is 'historically' accurate. However, we cannot put forward a case on the basis of this passage alone.

The last paragraph gives a relatively harmless example of the kind of pitfall which we need to avoid. There are other places where it becomes more vital that we do not take out of a passage more than we are supposed. Part of what will be done in this booklet is to try to take a careful look at biblical teaching on the subject of principalities and powers, avoiding issues that strictly belong to studies of personal or individual demonization.

Different views of 'strategic level spiritual warfare'

How we do evangelism is partly influenced by our view of principalities and powers, because that view affects how we deal with them in our evangelism. In the last hundred years or so there have been two major approaches to the issue of principalities and powers which give rise to differing strategies to combat them.

[1] For booklets on deliverance and demonization you are advised to consult either of the two following works. John Richards, *Exorcism, Deliverance and Healing*; (Grove Ministry and Worship series no.44) Graham Dow. *Those Tiresome Intruders* (Grove Pastoral series no.41).

These approaches have been, on the one hand, to see principalities and powers as powerful demonic spirits which I shall label 'demonic super-powers'. On the other hand they have been seen as symbols of human social and political structures.

Socio-political symbols
The approach which sees principalities and powers as social and political symbols has tended to characterize liberal and radical theologians. Such people have, not unnaturally, seen spiritual warfare as chiefly about social and political liberation, and evangelism has had to find a home (if at all) within that framework of thinking.

Demonic superpowers
The demonic superpower approach has tended to be the one taken by theologically conservative Christians. Within the conservative camp two views have developed as to how one deals with principalities and powers for the purposes of evangelism.[1] They differ with regard to the methods of combat recommended. One advocates direct engagement of principalities and powers in a manner similar to deliverance ministry and will be labelled 'direct engagement'. The other sees our engagement with principalities and powers in terms of the church fulfilling its mission to evangelize, heal, reveal God's love etc. This we shall call 'the classical view'. Let's look at these in more detail.

The direct engagement view[2]
In this school of thought, principalities and powers are viewed as highranking spirits in a total hierarchy of demons. Each demon assigned to rule places, ethnic groups, institutions etc. Their chief aim is to blind minds to the gospel (2 Cor. 4.4). In order to combat thse spirits they first need to be identified by research and prayer. Correct identification enables Christians to approach them directly in order to bind them in Jesus' name and so break their power. In this view such activity is a prerequisite to other ministries including evangelism.

The classical view
This view finds no scriptural warrant for many of the direct engagement claims and points to the sure warrants we have in scripture for advancing the Kingdom by preaching, prayer, evangelism, deliverance of individuals, healing and so on. These things, it is argued, are spiritual warfare in themselves.

A third way
There is a third approach which believes that principalities and powers are neither entirely spiritual, nor entirely earthly.[3] Re-examining the language used for power in the NT, it finds that principalities and powers are some-times seen as earthly 'powers', sometimes heavenly or spiritual, and often as both. This is the basic approach of this booklet and will be argued in the following pages. However, there are many things to be learnt from the other approaches and views. I hope to draw them together into a fuller picture.

[1] Lloyd Pietersen, *Shadows of Demons* in *Today* Magazine, May 1990.
[2] This approach is well expounded in Peter Adam, *Preparing for Battle* (Kingsway, 1987).
[3] Walter Wink, *Naming the Powers*. Lesslie Newbigin, *The Gospel in a Pluralist Society*. Nigel Wright, *The Fair Face of Evil*.

2. NEW TESTAMENT VIEWPOINTS

We shall examine some of the main New Testament passages which deal with spiritual warfare and relate to principalities and powers. Space prevents a detailed look at each passage, but the salient points are as follows.

2 Corinthians 10.1-6—demolishing strongholds

Here, Paul is warning he may have to discipline some of the church when he returns to Corinth. The reason is that some of the Corinthian Christians are being led astray. He calls for action to rescue and to save them. Paul sees such action as part of what we tend to call 'spiritual warfare'. It is for this reason that this passage is important.

Paul wants to emphasize that the war is for hearts, minds and allegiance. It is not about point-scoring and jockeying for popularity. Therefore he gives his effort to helping people to be transformed in their thinking so that they think, and therefore act, 'Christ-fully'. 'Taking every thought captive, obedient to Christ' does not mean ceasing to think!.

There are arguments and pretensions that become strongholds for resisting the spread of the knowledge of God; they stop people coming to understand and respond to the gospel. We recognize these in the philosophies or attitudes of the world around us. Most Christians are quick to spot and resist humanist atheism, but how many recognize the consumerism which tells us that fulfilment lies in acquiring more of the trappings of western wealth and which seeks to win over the church in its theological guise of prosperity teaching? How many resist the individualism of our society, which afflicts our churches by encouraging a split between life and faith? All too often western Christians can be consumerists on Saturday and Christians on Sunday. People need to be brought to see that they are more than customers or units of sale. In God's eyes they are more precious and in Christ can have a greater destiny. Their worth is in God's love for them, not in how prosperous they can become.

These strongholds will be brought down with divine weapons. Given that the strongholds are related to the way people see themselves and the world, we deduce that the weapons are brought to bear on minds and wills. This seems to show that the weapons are prayer and the proclaiming of the gospel. It is in line with what we discover in other passages relating to spiritual warfare. The battle is for the mind and allegiance, and the gospel is a primary weapon in that battle.

2 Corinthians 4.1-12—suffering for the gospel

It is the aim of 'the god of this age' to prevent people from understanding the gospel (v.4) so it was not necessarily a problem with the proclamation when people did not respond. Paul's problem was with the receptivity of his hearers which had been sabotaged by the devil. Quite clearly for Paul, spiritual warfare relates directly to evangelism.

Paul goes on to describe his ministry of setting forth the truth in terms which remind us of Jesus's own ministry, of suffering, of death and of resurrection. The purpose of such a ministry of suffering is to make Jesus known (4.7ff). In this passage we are reminded that it is not only by word and prayer that God uses us to shed the light of his gospel, but also by commitment that endures hardship and suffering for the sake of the gospel.

Spiritual warfare issues in Colossians

There are important things to learn regarding principalities and powers in Colossians and we will mainly consider 1.17ff and 2.8ff.

It would be easy, on a partial reading of the passages that deal with principalities and powers, to see them as basically evil and opposed to God in principle. Because of such a misreading, we might imagine that these powers only came into being as human society came under the sway of fallen angels or powerful demonic beings. However, Colossians reminds us that this is not quite so.

Paul reminds us how all things were created by Christ (1.16). This includes the spiritual realm, things invisible and 'thrones, powers, rulers, authorities'. These things were created for him. In other words, what we are calling 'principalities and powers' were *originally* created to serve the purposes of God.

Human societies are created and provided by God with structures and systems of organization which are intended to enable human beings to live together in peace, safety and good order (Rom. 13.1-7, 1 Tim. 2.1-4). Without them chaos and suffering follow. Remembering the events following the collapse of the Soviet Union should help us to avoid seeing principalities and powers in an entirely negative light. However, it becomes clear that these principalities and powers fell from their original place in God's purposes. Paul does not tell us at this point how this came about. He takes it as given that things in heaven needed to be reconciled to himself (1.20), and that Christ's cross and resurrection disarmed them (2.14-15).

Paul's desire for the Christians at Colossae was that they would have spiritual wisdom and understanding (1.11 and 2.2) so that they would continue to be fruitful Christians (1.10ff) whose effectiveness is not compromised by deceptive philosophies (2.4 and 8). In other words, Paul's concern was for the minds and allegiance of these Christians; that they should remain true to his preaching of the apostolic gospel which centres on Christ's supremacy and sufficiency. Note that the battle-ground is the heart and mind. We note also that the 'weapon' in view here is a right understanding, which is also called 'wisdom' or 'insight'.

We also need to grapple with what we learn from 2.8ff. Here we are introduced to the 'basic principles of this world'. The Greek underlying 'basic principles' is *stoicheia*. They are opposed to Christ in verse 8 and we see how the *stoicheia* were almost conceived of in personal terms. The context leads us to see them as another way of describing the powers and authorities of verses 10 and 15. These *stoicheia* seek to exercise control over human life. The Greek construction makes it clear that we are dealing with life-determining authority[1] and it is the same construction as used with 'Christ' in this verse. It is an authority which rightly belongs to Christ. The battle is for allegiance. who determines our life, Christ or the principalities and powers? This is the battleground of spiritual warfare, this is the arena of evangelism.

Paul goes on to affirm that Christ is the sole access to the whole fullness of God (as opposed to the claims of the Colossian 'New Agers'). Christ is the rightful head of the principalities and powers. The conclusion is clear; those who have been rescued from the dominion of darkness 'in Christ' share Christ's freedom from the principalities and powers. Our baptism demonstrates our position in Christ. we share in his death and resurrection. Verse 15 reminds us that on the cross the principalities and powers were taken on and defeated. This is our victory in Christ.

Colossians as related to the Gospels
In the Gospels there is nothing of the phrase 'principalities and powers'. Colossians gives us the clue as to where to look in the Gospels to find them. the cross. In the Easter events we see the principalities and powers defeated. Given what we know about them from their titles ('rulers, powers, authorities' etc) we can see them behind the events leading up to the crucifixion. We can see them in the vested interests of Jewish religion, in the politics of colonialism, and in the weaknesses of particular personalities under pressure. The principalities and powers conspired, through such means, to bring Jesus to the cross, but in God's plan this was to be the means of their defeat.

Principalities and powers were 'in' the politicking which brought Jesus to the cross. We can see them clearly in the social attitudes and institutions which Jesus's teaching and healing challenged. Those attitudes and institutions kept large sections of the population from the knowledge of God. We see principalities in the mounting opposition from the Pharisees and Sadducees arising mainly from their complicity in those attitudes and institutions. We see them in the power that is misused to crucify the Lord of Glory. We see them in the fear of the disciples when they were faced with all of this.

It is instructive to remember how Jesus came against these powers. He proclaimed the kingdom of God. He brought insightful application of the truth to the lives and situations he came across. He proceeded with strategic planning ('I must preach in the other towns also' Luke. 4.42-44). And lastly but not leastly, he taught by means of his own suffering. We must surely expect to have to do the same things.

Spiritual warfare issues in Ephesians
Probably the most frequently cited text on spiritual warfare is Eph. 6.10-17. Leslie Mitton in his commentary on Ephesians[2] reminds us that we

[1] See Eduard Lohse, *Colossians and Philemon* (Fortress, 1971).
[2] C. Leslie Mitton, *Ephesians* (MMS 1973).

should keep this passage in context as we try to undertand it. It is important to note that from 5.3 to 6.9 instruction is given concerning proper ethical behaviour, Christian uprightness and good relationships within the Christian community, between individuals and within families. The notes about spiritual warfare are the last section of these instructions, note the 'Finally' starting 6.10. We need to relate this section to the preceeding instructions.

We are reminded that there are spiritual dynamics at work that are subverting human society and especially Christian witness. Calling attention to this dimension of the struggle emphasizes that we need to look beyond personal sin and beyond mere social or ideological pressure (such as the dividing wall of hostility in chapter 2). The struggle is not just against 'flesh and blood', i.e. not essentially against human beings.

Sometimes we regard our wrongdoing only in terms of personal sin and the pressures of 'the world'. When we do so we fail to take account of how our wrongdoing may be caught up in something else which is manipulating or even empowering it. In other words it is possible to see principalities and powers using social and political pressures as well as individual sinfulness to subvert Christian witness.

It is too easy in dealing with this passage to get bogged down with the items of armour. What is being asked here is to relate the concept of being involved in a spiritual struggle to the idea of putting on Christ. The Ephesian Christians are asked to maintain integrity, an attitude of obedience to God, confidence in and willingness to share the gospel and confidence in God's provision, protection and character. We can infer that these are things that principalities and powers are undermining or subverting.

In addition we are told of more offensive 'armour'. 'The word of God', which seems to cover two related areas of meaning. the truth of the apostolic gospel as applied to the various situations in which Christians find themselves and the God-inspired insights into the spiritual realities facing us.

We are also reminded that prayer 'in the Spirit' must take a central place. That is prayer which is born out of God's own heart and reflecting his plans and strategies. Such prayer will include praying for other Christians and (see v.19) especially for those involved in evangelism, indicating importance of evangelism as part of the struggle. The (s)word and prayer point to the importance of discernment, since the word has to be applied to the situation and since prayer in the Spirit will involve one in discovering God's will. Discernment involves correctly understanding the nature and tactics of principalities and powers in any particular community so that tactics can be discerned to counter them.

From this passage we gather that spiritual warfare involves us in the struggle to maintain Christian life and witness which is worthy of the Lord. We are reminded that discerning prayer is important, especially prayer for the spread of the gospel. It is fair to draw the implication that evangelism (making known the mystery of the gospel) is at the cutting edge of spiritual warfare (v.15 and 19).

Let us also take note of what we are told about the enemy. We note that the words used ('rulers . . . authorities . . . powers') are words that could apply to merely earthly rulers, but here are qualified by the addition of 'spiritual forces of evil in the heavenly realms'.

In Ephesians we have already met the phrase 'heavenly realms'; 1.3 tells us that this is where we have been blessed in Christ with every spiritual blessing. Christ is seated at the right hand of God the Father (1.20), though we note (1.21) that Christ's position is far above every authority, power etc.. We are seated with Christ (2.6) so that we are able to make known to the rulers and authorities in the heavenly realms what God has accomplished (3.10). The heavenly realms is the dimension of reality where Christ meets with and equips us. It is also the arena of spiritual warfare, the spiritual flip-side of material existence. It is not a totally separate dimension in relation to tangible/visible existence, it is our lives and world seen from a spiritual viewpoint. It might help to compare it to the tips of icebergs floating in the sea. If the part visible from the surface is affected in any way we can be sure that corresponding things are taking place below the surface. These things would not be separate, but intimately linked. The effects can flow in either direction; to fire a torpedo at the base of an iceberg will inevitably have repercussions on the surface of the water and *vice versa*.

In Eph. 3.10 (taking 2.11ff as the context), we see that when Christians live out the gospel, it is then that principalities and powers can actually 'hear' what is being proclaimed. Until the point where people begin to throw off the bondage imposed on them by the principalities and powers, there is no point of contact between principalities and powers and the gospel. For the principalities and powers, actions speak louder than words. These things are not addressed directly, as if they were personal demons. The lack of direct address surely implies that their mode of being is different from personal demons, presumably because it is related to social and power structures rather than individual human beings.

In this we see the importance of living out the Christian life for evangelistic spiritual warfare. It is in living it out that the principalities and powers are challenged. It is in living it out that others see that there is another way to live and so can begin to respond to the gospel themselves. The threat to the principalities and powers is that they are changed or destroyed when this change of lifestyle takes place on a large scale.

We should also note the difference between principalities and powers and personal demons as shown in Ephesians. In the Gospels, demons know who Jesus is and the difficulty is to keep them quiet! In Ephesians, the principalities and powers don't know Jesus until the church makes the gospel known. This surely indicates that we are dealing with two separate kinds of being.

Spiritual Warfare issues in the book of Revelation

The difficulties and controversies surrounding the book of Revelation tend to militate against its use in understanding spiritual warfare. Yet it has some very important things to remind us of regarding this conflict and evangelism.[1] If you are unconvinced by the amillennialist approach of the present author you will not find any conclusions that rest exclusively on these texts or this approach to Revelation.

The general approach here is to regard the book of Revelation as essentially revealing truths about how things may be seen from the spiritual realm in the time between the first and second coming of Christ. Its method is to identify earthly things with images which tell us about their spiritual reality and status. Early on in the book we are introduced to this when we find John writing to the Angels of the churches. Each church is addressed as a spiritual entity rather than a merely human institution.

The whole book revolves around seeing reality in different facets or perspectives. We hear of the Lion of Judah but we 'see' the once-slain Lamb (5.5 and 6). We hear the number of the redeemed 144,000 (7.4), but we 'see' a multitude without number (7.9). These different perceptions explain or give a fuller understanding of the reality being considered. It is important to note, therefore, that these other 'dimensions' of reality are not separate realities or beings, for example, the Angels of the churches are not separate from the churches they 'represent'. They are in reality those churches seen from a particular viewpoint. The spiritual reality is but another dimension of the total reality.

The section of the book covered by chapters 11.19-15.4 shows world history from the perspective of spiritual conflict. In common with the other section it breaks down into seven 'scenes'. The first (11.19-13.1) gives an overview of the following scenes. The second (13.2-10), third (13.11-18), fourth (14.1-5) and fifth (14.6-13) tell us of the main forces in the battle. The sixth scene (14.14) talks of the close of battle. The seventh (15.2 ff.) is a song of victory, a scene of heaven. For our purposes, the first five scenes are the most important.

The first scene reveals the woman and the dragon. The child (Jesus) is only very briefly seen since the focus of interest is on the people of God i.e. the woman and her offspring and also as Michael. For this reason Christ's death and resurrection is dealt with only briefly, while its significance as spiritual warfare is pictured more fully (12.7-9). We note how the spiritual victory of God's people follows from the events of Jesus' life and indeed seems to stand where we would expect a description of Christ's victory. In this section we learn that Satan 'leads the whole world astray' (12.9). Yet he has been thwarted in his ambitions, having failed, been hurled down and defeated in his attempt to destroy God's people. His anger leads to further warfare against 'those who obey God's commandments and hold to the testimony of Jesus' (12.17). The next four scenes show us the beast from the sea, the beast from the land, the 144,000 and the three angels. These represent the four main forces in the war respectively; corrupt political/social power, false religion and ideology, the church, and the gospel. The beast from the sea, corrupt socio-political power, is idolatrous, anti-Christian, and blasphemous. The beast's aim is to carry forward

[1] Any reader wishing to follow up these points should refer to Michael Wilcock's *Revelation* (The Bible Speaks Today series, IVP, first published 1975).

the war against the saints (13.7) and to provide alternative worship foci (13.8). It is supported by the beast 'out of the earth', false ideology/religion. The function of this beast is to give religious/ideological support and so apparent legitimacy to the first beast. This is achieved through deception (13.14) and coercion (13.14-17).

Arraigned against the bestial double force are the 144,000 and the three angels. The 144,000 represent the whole church in all ages. The three angels proclaim repentance, judgment and warning to the people of the earth and so may be taken as standing for the proclamation of the truth of the gospel as against the false religion/ideology of the second beast. It is important to note that the proclamation of the gospel is part of the equation of spiritual warfare. Proclamation is the means of winning people for God by exposing the truth about God and the beasts, by warning of the true state of affairs in the world, in the light of the End. To put it more sharply, evangelism is itself spiritual warfare.

The New Testament and Spiritual Warfare. the story so far.
The language relating to principalities and powers is imprecise and unsystematic. There are a number of terms in use and they seem to be used unspecifically. We have also seen that the use of such terms as 'principality', 'power', 'thrones' or 'dominions' is such that one or two words can stand for the whole class. The demands of context or argument seem to determine the usage rather than any system or supposed hierarchy or organization.[1] Therefore, we are quite at liberty to look at the whole set of terms as one class without trying to force distinctions onto the individual terms.

In addition we need to remember how these terms cover both physical and spiritual aspects of reality. They refer to a power structure in its widest definition, from human beings through social structures and authority systems to the spiritual dimensions of that power structure. In any one case the context may determine the focus, whether it is material or spiritual. In the absence of other words or grammatical constructions which might delimit the meaning, the widest sense is to be preferred. Sometimes human rulers or governmental systems are meant, sometimes the spiritual aspect is primary while in yet other places both aspects are included. In fact, early Christians would not have made the sharp distinction that we do between material and spiritual dimensions of power. For them it was all part of the picture, a view which they largely shared with their non-Christian contemporaries. This viewpoint is why the terms are so fluid and, from our point of view, hard to interpret.

Summary
Principalities and powers are not simply super-powerful spiritual entities differing only in magnitude from the personal demons found in the Gospels. In the Gospels the demons have to be silenced because they know who Jesus is, and yet when we deal with principalities and powers we note how they do not appear to know who he is (e.g. 1 Cor. 2.6-8 and Eph. 3.10). From this it seems that we are dealing with different categories of beings; on the one hand demons and on the other principalities and

---

[1] See Walter Wink's *Naming the Powers* for a thorough and convincing survey of this and following points.

powers.[1] We should also note that unlike the devil and all his angels, principalities and powers will one day be restored (Col. 1.16 and 20) rather than destroyed. So we need not worry that this interpretation does away with the demonic altogether; we need rather to think of principalities and powers as whole entities which are power/authority structures, having both human and spiritual poles of existence. We are back to the iceberg illustration; some of it above and some below the water.

It might be helpful to see how this might apply in a life situation. There is a certain 'spirit' which any institution has, perhaps a school, a soccer team, a supermarket chain, or a hospital. This 'spirit' is related to the people present in an institution, especially the more prestigious and powerful people. It relates to the laws and rules governing the institution, its customs, tradition, and roles. These rules, traditions etc. are shaped by the history of the institution and its goals. All of these help support an 'ethos'—a spiritual dimension. That other dimension which seems to govern and uphold the whole ethos of the institution and which is even bigger than its cultural identity is the 'spirit'. Some people sense this when they walk in or join the school, hospital etc. They can 'feel' the 'atmosphere'. I think part of what they are sensing is the 'angel', 'principality' or 'spirit' of the institution.

We should make two further observations about this before moving on. First, this 'angel'/'spirit' cannot be located separately in space-time from the institution or human group it corresponds to: it is tangible only in and through the group or institution. It has no separate existence; no point where it can be addressed directly except in the material forms it takes. This is why we have to be reminded that we are not really wrestling against flesh and blood. The people we face are not the problem on their own. It is the group, the corporate including the 'spiritual dynamic', rather than individuals who live or work within it. Our concern has to be to liberate the people, not defeat them.

Second, in our dealings with people we run the risk of 'getting personal' because we are dealing with persons and so we need to be reminded of the bigger picture. The person can and should be separated, to a degree, from the role. Without a queen, a monarchy may still continue through her heirs exercising the role in accordance with law, custom and tradition. So we cannot afford to focus overmuch on personalities when greater issues are at stake. This is not to say that personalities are irrelevant, but that without their power-base/ role/ position they are a different proposition. We need rather to wrestle with the whole thing, principalities and powers and spiritual forces of evil.

We have seen how Spiritual Warfare is waged. by prayer, by insightful understanding of the spiritual issues, by proclaiming the gospel, by right action and by commitment to living out the gospel to the point of suffering

---

[1] This differs from Wink, who extends the principle of his interpretation of principalities and powers to demons and Satan; seeing them merely as spiritual correlates of evil as it afflicts human individuals. Yet in the Gospels they react to, and know Jesus (unlike principalities etc.).

and even death. When this happens, principalities and powers are affected and people are freed to serve Christ. They can then relate properly to the structures and 'spiritualities' that order their lives. They need no longer idolize them (knowingly or otherwise) but see them as part of God's providence and seek to recall them to their God-given tasks of meeting human need, both physical and spiritual.

Principalities, powers and demons

Given the case argued so far that the demonic and the powers have different kinds of being, it is a fair question to ask what might be the relationship between the demonic and the powers. Part of the answer is suggested in an article by F. Douglas Pennoyer[1] on his work among the Tawbid in the Philipines. His starting point is that demonization is a personal relationship, presumably between a demon and a human being. His article shows the effect of demonization on a society and its culture. This happens by demonized individuals influencing and reinforcing certain ways of thinking and acting because they occupy socially or politically influential positions. It is easy to extrapolate this principle into other cultures. The demonic influence of key personalities can be a fulcrum to move a whole culture away from the gospel. Whether or not it is actually true that Hitler was into the Occult, the example of Nazism in pre-war Germany provides an insight into how this could be.

It is possible that such demons might claim for themselves grandiose titles, but their power is strategic rather than inherent. It would also explain apparent territoriality; such demons would be unhappy to leave areas where they know they have or can gain power and influence. This lack of territoriality would mean that they do not necesarily have some hierarchical structure to fit into. Their placing may be opportunistic.

The implication of such opportunism is that there may be times when a decisive strategic battle may be won by the Church when demonised individuals are delivered. But it probably will still require that the whole principality issue is addressed. If it is not, there may still be opportunity for the overtly demonic to set up house and re-deploy its influence.

---

[1] C. Peter Wagner and F. Douglas Pennoyer (eds.), *Wrestling with Dark Angels* (Monarch, 1990).

3. PUTTING IT ALL TOGETHER

Earlier in this booklet we looked at three approaches to the issue of spiritual warfare and evangelism. the 'direct engagement' view, the classic view (that the powers are demonic but not to be directly engaged), and the view that they are not inherently demonic and are to be treated accordingly. It should now be clearer why the third approach is to be preferred. The NT does not encourage us to see principalities and powers simply as demonic beings or merely as a way of describing human social or political structures. In this section we shall look more closely at these different approaches in order to refine their valuable insights.

A critique of the direct engagement viewpoint
It is hard to know with the 'direct engagement' view how to address the principalities and powers. If the model is deliverance of an individual then the question must be asked; 'To whom, or to where do we go to find the spirit to address?' If we decide to approach a particular place, how do we know that such a spirit is there and listening? Indeed, how do we know what effect our words or actions may have had? In reflecting on these questions it must be noted that there have been many actions and words which have been based on this approach which have failed to make the kind of impact that might have been expected following this theory. Numerous 'Marches for Jesus' have failed to make any significant impact on the spiritual atmosphere of this land, though they have achieved many other good things. On their own they have failed to produce the results that the direct-engagement theory would lead us to expect. It is interesting to note that many seem to be moving away from this view, perhaps as they see that it doesn't yield the predicted harvest.

Further questions arise from the lack of clear biblical warrant for this approach. The lack of scriptural basis has been the objection which proponents of the classic view have made, emphasizing that we deal with principalities and powers by praying, evangelizing and living out the gospel. It is a valid objection, though perhaps inconsistent since they treat demons and principalities and powers differently despite affirming that they are essentially alike. We do not find a scriptural precedent or injunction for a direct, verbal approach to principalities and powers. Nor is there any record of events such as 'praise marches' or other 'direct engagements' as a run-up to church planting or evangelism. Indeed it seems, from what we have seen of the NT evidence, that the classic viewpoint is right. the whole enterprise of mission is spiritual warfare. Spiritual warfare is not a separate activity which precedes evangelism.

'Direct engagers' might want to reply that research and prayer should reveal the likely locations of principalities and powers. However, experience shows that this is not the case. Indeed the biblical evidence we have examined would suggest that such a search is futile. We cannot engage the principalities and powers without dealing with their material aspects, without getting stuck into mission and all it entails. I wonder whether the direct engagement view arises partly out of a desire for quick-fix solutions to our evangelistic challenges. This desire could be a reflection of our culture's pursuit of the instant, the easy and the commitment-free. For, if we could evangelize like this, it would seem at first sight to offer relatively instant success without all the hard work of relationship-building, planning, mission strategy and changed lifestyle.

The other thing to be wary of in this approach is whether it feeds a need to have an enemy. It can be a good feeling to exercise 'righteous anger'. It is easier to mobilize support and enthusiasm if there is an enemy to fight. And perhaps, if we are not careful, what this approach does is allow people to feel that they are fighting really important battles, without cost, risk or real involvement. I hope this reflection is cynical, but I make it because I fear it is not. In the light of the biblical material it is, at the least, praying in a fantasy world.

Some hard cases from the direct engagement camp

It would not be fair to dismiss the approach which builds on the idea of personal demonic ruling spirits without wrestling with the strong points of the case. In this instance the strong argument is not scriptural but practical. Despite the apparent failure of the direct engagement approach, there is evidence from 'the field' suggesting that the territorial/sociopolitical spirit is a reality and this lends credence to the approach.

Peter Wagner has collected some of the instances of encounters with territorial spirits as part of his attempt to get the whole issue opened up properly.[1] It is some of these we will now consider.

In his article, 'Territorial Spirits', Wagner mentions how conversions in Thailand followed the setting aside of one day a week for 'spiritual warfare'. He mentions the strange case of the Brazil/Uruguay border town where on the Uruguayan side of the street a person may be resistant to the gospel, but where the same person, on crossing to the Brazilian side, may become open to evangelism. In Argentina, Omar Cabrera identifies the spirits of cities and breaks their power before embarking on evangelistic campaigns, subsequently finding little resistance to the gospel. Mention is also made of the case of a demonically inspired mental illness being unable to follow the patient from Costa Rica to the USA. These examples all suggest territoriality and are advanced to show how spirits may control or be restricted to certain territories.

What are we to make of such things? First of all, we must be wary of building doctrine on experience rather than Scripture. God in his mercy may (and often does) choose to use our prayers and efforts despite our theology or practice. Hence, despite the actual method of prayer that may have been used in Thailand, God may have chosen to use the prayer and humble seeking of his will to significantly advance the gospel. The answer does not necessarily endorse the pattern of prayer in this case. Praying in biblically unfounded ways cannot be justified on pragmatic grounds alone, e.g. praying to dead saints!.[2] This applies also to the Omar Cabrera case. In his case it would be helpful to know more about the situation in Argentina; what has been the experience of other evangelists working there? Does their experience differ? What precisely is meant by 'breaking its power'? Given that the situation in Argentina appears to be very open to the gospel, is it not possible that similar results might be acheived if Sr. Cabrera prayed in a different way?

[1] C. Peter Wagner (ed). *Territorial Spirits* (Sovereign World 1991)
[2] I am aware that there is a difference theologically between praying to saints and asking the dead for their prayers, whatever one's view of the advisability of the latter.

The situation on the Brazil/Uruguay border is interesting but it need not affect significantly the approach I have been outlining. The human psychology and social identity is complex and the spirtual dimension of a nation or state is real. The interaction of these factors may be quite sufficient to give rise to the phenomenon outlined. I would guess that the combination may well have a lot to do with the mental illness case, that the important factor is not the demon's 'turf' (though see comments above at the end of the NT section) but the person's inner response to place. Indeed demonic 'territoriality' may be related to the spiritual dynamics of human institutions. It would bear further investigation but presents no apparent difficulty in principle to the thesis of this booklet.

One widely-quoted example of spiritual warfare in evangelism is used to illustrate the importance of taking the warfare dimension seriously. It seems to point towards the understanding developed in this booklet. The incident took place in the city of Cordoba, Argentina, during the 1978 World Cup finals. YWAM were attempting to evangelize but not very successfully. So, they held a prayer retreat during which the true nature of the battle was revealed. The city was being ruled by a 'demonic principality' of pride which had become, they understood, immersed in the culture of the city leading to a over-valuing of position, possessions and appearance. They understood that this could only be overcome by humility. So they went onto the streets and malls and physically prostrated themselves before God in prayer for the city. This proved to be the breakthrough, and immediately crowds gathered who wanted to know about Christ and turn to him.

The important thing is the way the principality was engaged. It was not by some form of corporate exorcism or authority-taking, but rather by a changed attitude and obedience. The change in people's attitudes came about when they saw demonstrated the gospel spirit opposed to the spirit of pride. Their perceptions were challenged and the lie of the enemy began to be exposed, a lie that had lain entrenched in the corporate spirituality of the city.

Useful insights from direct-engagers

Even though unconvinced about the way that principalities and powers are viewed, I believe there are some important insights to be treasured which hold true and make sense within a more fully biblical framework.

John Wimber, who is not a follower of the direct engagement line of thought, described how a Vineyard team, preparing to minister in Australia, were made aware that there was a spirit of rejection and inferiority at work hindering Australians from knowing the power of the gospel. They tackled this by praying for that area of people's lives to be opened up to the gospel and by preaching with the knowledge of that spirit in mind. John Wimber described his prayer at this time as 'Lord, shed the light of the truth of your word wherever we go. Demolish the stronghold of rejection through the clear teaching and reception of grace.'[1]

In this example we see the value of identifying a power's characteristic hindrance to the gospel and basing our intercession on that identification. The binding of the strong man takes place when we pray this way. It is not some kind of magical formula. Binding takes place as we pray in the Spirit, responding to his leading and revelation.

[1] *Equipping the Saints* magazine, vol. 4 issue 1.

4. EVANGELISTIC SPIRITUAL WARFARE
AN ECLECTIC GUIDE TO ACTION

The aim of this section is to build up a series of guidelines for taking the principalities and powers dimension of evangelism seriously in a way that should enhance the work of the local church and without fantasy. The guidelines are eclectic in the sense that it will take insights from the different approaches and to use all that can be usefully pressed into service. It is my conviction that many ideas can be wrong and yet have power or credibility because they are actually based on true insights wrongly developed.

One of the valuable things that emerges from the 'direct engagement camp' is a methodology for identifying the characteristics of principalities and powers. While the style of dealing with principalities and powers may be open to question, the fact that they take the issue seriously has led to the development of an approach which can be helpful in getting the measure of the spiritual battle and so contribute to winning spiritual battles.

Worship as spiritual warfare
The biblical precedent for using worship in spiritual warfare is 2 Chron. 20.21 and 22. This may not be the best basis to build on. The passage is a frequently used text in this connection, but probably it is misused because the context is ignored. All too often a theology of praise as a spiritual weapon is built on this text. In fact it was the obedience of the people to the command of God given by the prophecy of Jahaziel which won the day. The praise was mainly an expression of confidence that the battle was the Lord's. It was not explicitly commissioned by God. If anything, we should learn from this incident that it is faith and trust in God that is the 'weapon' here. Praise is not a weapon in scripture, praise is what God deserves and is directed to him.

However, this does not remove the validity and importance of praise in situations of spiritual conflict. John Dawson[1] outlines another good reason why we should start and set aside opportunities for praise. The reason he gives is that praise and thanksgiving, and the attitude behind worship are good counterweights to the sins of complaint and murmuring. An attitude of complaint darkens our spirits, Dawson says, and makes us less able to receive God's words for the blessing of our cities. Revelation comes to the grateful because gratitude fosters humility and humility makes people more open to God's revelation.

Those who murmur usually do so on a basis of supposed rights which have not been yielded to God. On the basis of the preceding paragraph we need to ask ourselves what our attitude is to our city (or any locality to which we belong) and to exercise the discipline of praise in regard to it. It seems right to follow his advice in this, after all the Jewish exiles were

[1] John Dawson, *Taking our Cities for God* (Word, 1989).

told, through Jeremiah, to seek the peace of their city of exile (Jer. 29.7). It seems to me that we also should cultivate a praising and grateful attitude because it helps keep us fixed on God and his greatness and love, both of which we need to be sure of in order to minister most effectively.

The importance of waiting on God
Another aspect is to wait on God. The importance of this should be obvious. It is God's battle and we depend on him for the tactics and resources to fight. Anything more is presumptuous, possibly dangerous, and certainly a recipe for ineffectiveness.

Identify with the area's sin
A further step is to identify with the area's sin. This step touches something of God's broken-heartedness e.g. Jer. 8.19ff. This identification should culminate in personal and corporate repentance. It may at first seem difficult to make this identification, but usually we can find within ourselves the root of any given sin if not the actual sin. Dawson gives an example of abortion. We may not have experienced an abortion, yet we can all see within ourselves at least one of the contributory sins. lust, love of comfort, rejection, love of money, unbelief. These sins are the ones we would need to confess and turn from.

Living in the opposite spirit
The corporate repentance just mentioned gives rise to the next step which is to overcome evil with good, or (in YWAM parlance) 'to live in the opposite spirit'. Living in an opposite spirit requires that we identify the spiritual oppression that faces our neighbours and then find the right positive actions/lifestyle to resist that enemy stronghold. If it is consumerism we must find ways to resist that spirit in our own lives, perhaps by adopting simple and non-status lifestyles. If it is greed, we must cultivate generosity. A lifestyle change like these has the effect of 'declaring' to the principalities and powers that Jesus is Lord. To our neighbours it can show the possibility of liberation for them and even begin to sow seeds of their own repentance.

Stickability
The last thing is simply to continue until a breakthrough is reached. Sticking at it is the hardest part. To weather the set-backs, to carry the burden of concern laid upon us by the Holy Spirit right through until the end is difficult. There is no quick fix here. Our commitment is called for, lives laid down in submission and sacrifice are required. To keep at something for the sake of the gospel is spiritual warfare; involving our loyalties, our lifestyles and our own liberation. Only in this way can we really engage principalities and powers, bind them and plunder their houses.

Naming the Powers
The key lies in identifying the nature of the hold of principalities and powers on our neighbours and often on ourselves as well. A starting place for making this identification is to undertake historical and social research into the origins and development of your city or region. Of course, such research needs to be done with prayer so as not to exclude the Holy Spirit. God may use such study to alert us to or help us see what spiritual

dynamics are at work. I use the term 'spiritual dynamics' because it conveys the idea of an influence with shaping power. The word 'dynamic' has to do with power, and perhaps the term conveys more accurately to modern minds something of what we should understand by 'principalities and powers'. Research gives us a way to begin to approach our evangelism bearing principalities and powers in mind.

First of all we need to encourage someone to research the history of the community with a view to discovering recurrent trends and patterns which may be significant from a spiritual viewpoint. They should try to find out what God's purpose might be for the community e.g. is it to be a place of learning, of commerce, of industry? Next they should discover whether this purpose has been perverted into prideful ways, greed, exploitation or some other evil. It is important also to look for any great sins committed which seem to bequeath their legacy to the present—perhaps a massacre such as York's massacre of the Jewish community in medieval times or child labour in industrial cities in the early industrial revolution. Sometimes such sins can cast a spiritual shadow over the subsequent history of a community. There is something like this in parts of the letters to the seven churches in the book of Revelation. We should remember too that for early Christians this process would have been relatively easy because the spiritual dynamics of their cities were often identified by its gods.

One modern example of principalities and powers working through history sometimes cited is how a suspected spirit of greed shown in the Californian gold rush still seems to dominate Los Angeles and San Francisco. Sometimes it can be restricted to a small area and its church; I know of a British church whose effectiveness in outreach has been recurrently marred by factionalism which seems to have its roots in strife between families or 'clans' stretching back many years. The strife often seems to be connected to dominant women and usually has the effect of cutting back the church's outreach. It may even be linked to the possibility that the pagan past of the area may have encouraged devotion to Ella, goddess of wells and springs.

In my own town of Halifax I am sure that churches working together is an important counterbalance to the religious rivalry that has marked periods of its history and that was etched into the skyline by the building of rival church spires.

In looking at the history, attention should be paid to geo-political and social influence, religious (including pagan) history and particular traumatic or beneficient foundational events. The result of this research should then be able to feed the thanksgiving, the repentance and lifestyle phases of the campaign.[1]

---

[1] See the books by John Dawson and Peter Adams, *op. cit.*

5. SOME OUTWORKING EXAMPLES

Here are three churches seeking to bring spiritual warfare principles into their evangelism. They are a hotch-potch of my own and other people's experiences and observations. Therefore the basic experiences are real-life. To protect confidentiality much has been changed. To make easier reading each example is actually an amalgam of several situations. It is hoped that the inclusion of real-life examples will help the examples to ring true. It must not however, be assumed that they give complete or reliable information about any one church.

Christchurch

This parish is set in a city suburb. Originally a farming and artisan community, it is being swallowed by the advance of the city. Having working class roots, it has become 'gentrified' and is becoming a fashionable area.

For Christchurch the issue of spiritual warfare started to arise in the preparation for a parish mission. As prayer support was being mobilized people in leadership began to be aware of various co-incidences of opposition or difficulty. They felt that they were not just dealing with flesh and blood but with spiritual opposition. Informally and without co-ordination, some people started to research the history of the area. Others began to pray about the kind of 'spiritual atmosphere' they felt. The result of this prayer and research was an increased awareness of the 'spiritual atmosphere' in Christchurch parish. One of the characteristics seemed to be 'Rivalry'. This spirit dynamic worked against the spread of the gospel in several ways. One of those ways was to keep the churches apart by competition, often focussing on spiritual trivia such as size of summer fair or numbers in the choir. As Christchurch had recently begun to grow the rivalry had reared its head within the church itself. Factionalism led to some very bitter and public fallings-out about apparently small matters. Such fallings-out led to a drop in the number of active members through disillusionment and it turned away a good many people 'ripe for evangelism' who were on the fringe.

Unfortunately this insight was not seen to be important by the church because of the *ad hoc* nature of the research and the lack of accountability to the formal leadership. With their full prayer-cover unharnessed, the mission went ahead with the usual slightly disappointing results. Those who had been most concerned with prayer felt that breakthrough point had not been reached with regard to the area as a whole. However, the problem was faced by the leaders when they reflected on the mission afterwards, and action is being taken. First of all this is done by sharing the ideas of 'strategic level spiritual warfare' with the church through a sermon series linked to teaching in housegroups. One of the objectives in the housegroups is to begin to identify those who seem to have intercessory gifts in order to equip and use them better.

Another action following from this has been to give proper recognition to the research and insights of the *ad hoc* group. This recognition was given by prayerfully checking over their insights with the leadership and trusted outsiders. The results are due to be presented as part of the teaching on the subject with the aim that ideas that can be moulded into a plan of action. One further outcome is that the church leadership is taking the idea of reconciliation more seriously, starting with praying for their 'rival' churches and seeking to build effective bridges at personal and institutional levels. Someone on the PCC has even suggested that the church considers spending a few months learning about how to handle conflict. This will be considered along with the other suggestions arising from housegroup discussions.

St. Ydobon's church
This parish is in a mining village close to a larger town. The area has had a coal-based economy since the mid-1800's. Lately this situation has been changing and unemployment is as high as confidence is low. A once stable community is beginning to experience massive social change.

Spiritual warfare got onto the agenda for this church following the visit to the area of a group teaching about healing ministry. During the visit the group felt constrained to address the issue of the history of the area from the point of view of its spiritual effects. This teaching encouraged some of St.Ybodon's members to begin to think and pray about the matter relating to their own community.

The visiting group had suggested that the use of child labour in the mines and the callous treatment of workers and their families by the original land (and mine) owners had generated a spirit of resentment. Some of this resentment was shown now in the present-day resentful attitude of the general community to the church—a church which had tacitly given its blessing to what its loyal and wealthy sons were doing and had benefited materially from the wealth of the mines. For many people this resentment went beyond a mere 'us and them' feeling to a non-rational feeling that the church was a predatory institution—out to deprive them of their rights. An attempt at baptismal reform blew up much more hurtfully because it was seen as an attempt to deprive children of their right to be christened. The gospel issue behind it was obscured by the resentment.

Having accepted that there might well be something in this, St.Ybodon's wanted to take this further and this was when the trouble began. A disagreement arose as to the next step. There were those who suggested that a powerful demonic spirit of Resentment was the cause. Then there were those who felt that talk of demons was a bit over the top and that social forces and upbringing were the real issue. The Vicar did not want to deny the reality of the demonic, but felt that he wanted to give a bit more credence to the social dimension than the first group were doing. Moreover, to fail to endorse one view or the other would be interpreted as selling out to the other side, in one case to be written off as a skeptical liberal or, in the other, as some raving fundamentalist.

Needing the wisdom of a serpent and gentleness of a dove he prayed and called in prayer support from a number of people who had been a support group for him over the years. After reflection and advice he felt that he needed to bring the two groups together to try to reach some common understanding and a way to deal with their differences constructively. It seemed to him that, despite the 'theoretical' differences, there were many areas where in practice there was little or no conflict. He asked trusted members of each group to tell him how they saw things and to share their worries about the position of the other group. This was followed up with a meeting for everyone where he tried to interpret each position to the other group, and then mapped out the areas of agreement, and tried to give a perspective that both groups might be able to go along with.

The church was able therefore, to agree that the social/historic problem had an effect on people's spiritual responses and could thus be thought of as having a spiritual dimension. Obviously one group wanted to go further than that but they were willing to accept a conscientious difference. They also agreed that the way to deal with this 'spiritual dynamic' was by mobilizing prayer directed to dealing with this 'spirit' of resentment.

In the fulness of time the two groups became less distinct. The idea of a demonic element became less threatening to many of the 'liberal' group, while the other group became less uneasy about the idea that much of the spiritual dynamic was not necessarily demonic, accepting that there may be a scriptural distinction between demons and principalities and powers. Later on, the church was able, unitedly, to organize a series of prayer walks round different districts of the parish each led by one or two of the congregation who lived there. Another outcome was that a monthly meeting was organized to pray about the issues. At one of the meetings they were led to organize a service of penitence in Lent where the whole church could confess the sins of the area. As yet no decisive breakthrough has been reached but there is a trickle of people coming along to find out about the faith and the next PCC is to discuss starting a Christian basics strategy.

Saints and Martyrs
This church is known as S&M by its friends. The parish was formed in the heyday of the Victorian expansion of its manufacturing town by one of the town's major entrepreneurs and benefactors. It is a working class district with patches of suburban housing. The town used to rely on the cloth trade but now after a period of slump is diversifying. The area is becoming very socially mobile and the residents more rootless.

Facing an area traditionally hardened against the gospel, church leaders began to feel that they needed to address the underlying causes of decline. Increasingly, it was felt, this meant looking into principalities and powers as a way to back up the work of 'Pencaster for Christ'. So they began to look into the matter and to approach it systematically. This decision resulted in a small group of people researching the social and economic history of the area. The group members were themselves 'covered' by the prayer of others as they did this work. At the same time plans began to be laid for teaching and prayer events to help congregations in the area be aware of the 'strategic level' dimension of prayer.

One of the tasks the study group found themselves doing was finding a way for Christians who held differing views of spiritual warfare to be able to pray together. There were some who were only too happy to be rebuking spirits left right and centre, while others were very reluctant to recognize the demonic at all. Recognizing the importance of intercession, action and lifestyle gave a way in that could be accepted by all. All likewise acknowledged the importance of identifying and dealing with the underlying spiritual dimension to the gospel-hindrances they met.

The result of the study group's research and prayer was the discovery that the industrialization of the area had left vast sections of the population (mostly working class) with only tenuous links with organized religion. The workers despaired of their working conditions. The churches were unable or unwilling to help them. The effects of the enlightenment were soaking into the social, political and cultural soil. All of this nurtured a materialistic 'spirit' whose creed could aptly be summed up in the words; 'eat, drink and be merry, for tomorrow we die'. Hope lay in achieving material prosperity or at the bottom of a glass or three. Another discovery was that child labour had been used in the early part of the industrial revolution, and that the conditions of work were callous and shameful in terms of hours and conditions. It was felt that the spirit of this exploitation was still living on in the treatment of children in many parts of the borough, where they were often neglected and treated as annoying baggage.

The area had many good things. It had been the cradle of much inventiveness and had nurtured a fine caring tradition in its institutions and responsible local government. The ideas of nurturing were felt to be important. Something of God's purposes for the area was thought to be seen in the inventiveness and caring. The perversion of this had come with the abuses of capitalism and the slide into hedonism which had begun to undermine the caring and community aspects of the area.

These 'results' of prayerful research were shared with church leaders and comment and further reflection invited. The result was that most church leaders agreed that they would proceed on the basis of the analysis offered by the group and so began to use them as a basis for action. The findings were fed into teaching and prayer events. Many sensed that they ought to be addressing the issue on the level of lifestyle and so encouragement was also given for people to review their lifestyles in the light of what teaching about the principalities of the area. Particularly important was the call to a simpler lifestyle and one in which caring for others could be much more prominent. Churches were also encouraged to set up projects and events which could help foster a sense of community.

A quarterly prayer meeting was arranged to bring the churches together. At one of the early meetings a time of corporate repentance for the sin and thanksgiving for God's goodness in the district was held. Prayer was focussed on the materialistic hedonism of the area; asking particularly that people would become more urgently aware of the unsatisfying nature of materialism and of their own restlessness without God.

Because many in S&M could now see the wealth issue in a mission perspective the simple lifestyle message was being heard in an unprecedented way. The church leadership had prepared the ground carefully by taking care to listen to the questions and anxieties of the